WASHINGTON, DC

The Nation's Capital

BY
JOHN HAMILTON

Abdo & Daughters

An imprint of Abdo Publishing | abdopublishing.com

abdopublishing.com

Published by ABDO Publishing, a division of ABDO, PO Box 398166, Minneapolis, Minnesota 55439. Copyright © 2017 by Abdo Consulting Group, Inc. International copyrights reserved in all countries. No part of this book may be reproduced in any form without written permission from the publisher. ABDO & Daughters™ is a trademark and logo of ABDO Publishing.

Printed in the United States of America, North Mankato, Minnesota.
082016
092016

Editor: Sue Hamilton   **Contributing Editor:** Bridget O'Brien
Graphic Design: Sue Hamilton
Cover Art Direction: Candice Keimig   **Cover Photo Selection:** Neil Klinepier
Cover Photo: iStock
Interior Images: Alamy, AP, Cliff, D.C. United, Dreamstime, Frode Jacobsen, George Beck, Getty, Georgetown University, Granger, iStock, Library of Congress, Mike Davy, Mile High Maps, NASA, National Archives, New York Public Library, Ronald Reagan Washington National Airport, Science Source, Smithsonian, Washington Capitals, Washington Metropolitan Area Transit Authority/Larry Levine, Washington Mystics, Washington Nationals, Washington Redskins, Washington Wizards, White House/Pete Souza & Lawrence Jackson, White House Historical Association/Tom Freeman, Wikimedia, and William Russell Birch.

Statistics: *State and City Populations*, U.S. Census Bureau, July 1, 2015 estimates; *Land and Water Area*, U.S. Census Bureau, 2010 Census, MAF/TIGER database; *State Temperature Extremes*, NOAA National Climatic Data Center; *Climatology and Average Annual Precipitation*, NOAA National Climatic Data Center, 1980-2015 statewide averages; *State Highest and Lowest Points*, NOAA National Geodetic Survey.

Websites: To learn more about the United States, visit booklinks.abdopublishing.com. These links are routinely monitored and updated to provide the most current information available.

Cataloging-in-Publication Data

Names: Hamilton, John, 1959- author.
Title: Washington, DC / by John Hamilton.
Description: Minneapolis, MN : Abdo Publishing, [2017] | Series: The United
    States of America | Includes index.
Identifiers: LCCN 2015957746 | ISBN 9781680783513 (lib. bdg.) |
    ISBN 9781680774559 (ebook)
Subjects: LCSH: Washington (DC)--Juvenile literature.
Classification: DDC 975.3--dc23
LC record available at http://lccn.loc.gov/2015957746

CONTENTS

THE
NATION'S
CAPITAL

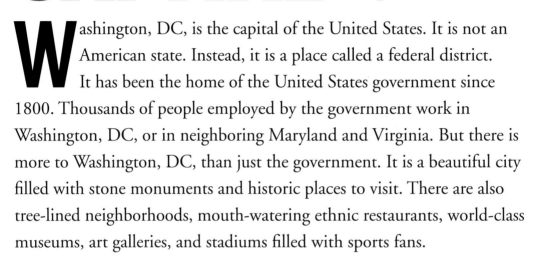

Washington, DC, is the capital of the United States. It is not an American state. Instead, it is a place called a federal district. It has been the home of the United States government since 1800. Thousands of people employed by the government work in Washington, DC, or in neighboring Maryland and Virginia. But there is more to Washington, DC, than just the government. It is a beautiful city filled with stone monuments and historic places to visit. There are also tree-lined neighborhoods, mouth-watering ethnic restaurants, world-class museums, art galleries, and stadiums filled with sports fans.

Washington, DC, is nicknamed "DC," or "the District." It is named after George Washington, the nation's first president. The DC part stands for "District of Columbia." Columbia was a popular, poetic name for the United States in the 1700s and 1800s. The word refers to Christopher Columbus, the European explorer who sailed to North America in 1492.

A statue of George Washington in Washington, DC. He was leader of the Continental Army and America's first president. The city is named for him.

QUICK FACTS

Name: Washington is named after President George Washington. District of Columbia is named after Christopher Columbus.

Date of Creation: Founded on July 16, 1790. The United States government officially moved to the city in 1800.

Population: 672,228

Area (Total Land and Water): 68 square miles (176 sq km)

Nicknames: DC, or the District

Motto: *Justitia omnibus* (Justice To All)

Official Bird: Wood Thrush

American Beauty Rose

Official Flower: American Beauty Rose

Official Tree: Scarlet Oak

Official Song: "The Star-Spangled Banner"

Scarlet Oak

Highest Point: Reno Reservoir in Tenleytown, 410 feet (125 m)

Lowest Point: Potomac River, 1 foot (.3 m)

Average July High Temperature: 88°F (31°C)

Record High Temperature: 106°F (41°C) on July 20, 1930

Average January Low Temperature: 24°F (-4°C)

Potomac River

Record Low Temperature: -15°F (-26°C) on February 11, 1899

Average Annual Precipitation: 41 inches (104 cm)

Number of U.S. Senators: 0

Number of U.S. Representatives: 0

U.S. Postal Service Abbreviation: DC

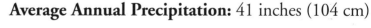

GEOGRAPHY

Washington, DC, is in the Middle Atlantic region of the United States. Its total land and water area is 68 square miles (176 sq km). It borders Maryland to the northwest, northeast, and southeast. The Potomac River runs along the southwestern side of the city. Across the river is the state of Virginia.

The Anacostia River flows through the southern part of the city in a northeast-to-southwest direction. It empties into the Potomac River. Three reservoirs supply water to the city. They include Dalecarlia, McMillan, and Georgetown Reservoirs. Many parts of the city were once wetlands.

Deciduous trees surround a creek in a Washington, DC, park.

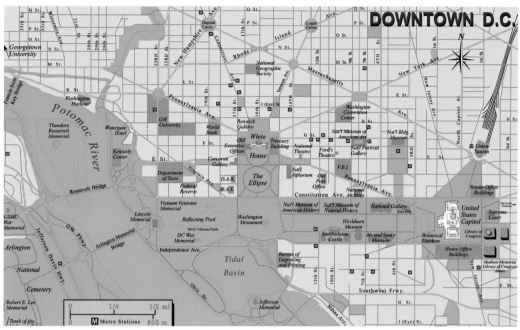

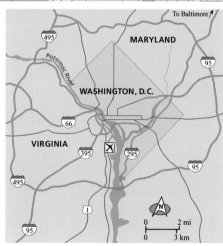

Washington, DC's total land and water area is 68 square miles (176 sq km). It is the capital of the United States.

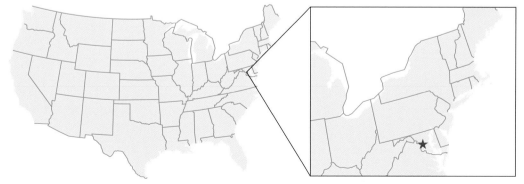

The highest spot in Washington, DC, is Reno Reservoir, in the neighborhood of Tenleytown, in the northwestern part of the city. It is 410 feet (125 m) above sea level. The lowest point in the city is along the Potomac River. It measures just 1 foot (.3 m) above sea level.

In the 1790s, the city of Washington was created within the federal District of Columbia. It was one of several settlements in the district. The district also included the villages of Georgetown and Alexandria, both of which were along the Potomac River. The new capital was created between these villages. At first, it was called the Federal City. In 1791, the name was changed to Washington to honor the nation's first president.

The Potomac River (top of photo) forms the city's southwestern border.

A satellite view of Washington, DC.

In 1791, George Washington appointed French architect Pierre L'Enfant to plan the layout of the city. L'Enfant decided that the Capitol building, where lawmakers would meet, should be in the center of the city. He then connected other important government buildings, such as the White House and the Supreme Court, with long, straight streets and diagonal avenues. The grid symbolized that the parts of the United States government were separate, but still connected with each other. L'Enfant also designed a wide strip of open parkland that is today the National Mall.

GEOGRAPHY

CLIMATE AND
WEATHER

Washington, DC, is in a climate zone called humid subtropical. There are four seasons, with hot, humid summers and cool winters. In summer, the average July high temperature is 88°F (31°C). The record high was a sweltering 106°F (41°C), which occurred on July 20, 1930. The region's heat and humidity often fuel thunderstorms. On rare occasions, the storms can be so strong that they spawn tornadoes.

Lightning strikes near the Washington Memorial.

Winters in Washington, DC, are usually mild. The average January low temperature is 24°F (-4°C). Temperatures that are below 0°F (-18°C) are very rare. The coldest temperature ever recorded in the city was -15°F (-26°C) on February 11, 1899.

The city receives a fair amount of precipitation. The average annual amount of rain and snow is 41 inches (104 cm). A typical winter brings about 15 inches (38 cm) of snow. Because average winter daytime temperatures are mild, most of the snow melts quickly.

Spring and fall are very pleasant in Washington, DC. The lower humidity and mild temperatures bring many tourists to the city during these seasons.

While rare, hurricanes sometimes make their way toward Washington, DC. Because the city is so far inland, hurricanes do little damage except for bringing heavy rains.

CLIMATE AND WEATHER

HISTORY

A wax figure of a Piscataway Indian.

Before European settlers came to the Washington, DC, area, Native American tribes had lived on the land for thousands of years. Members of the Piscataway tribe settled along the north side of the Potomac River, in present-day Maryland. They were an Algonquian-speaking people. Powhatan Indians lived on the south side of the river, in present-day Virginia. When Europeans came, the Native Americans were forced to move to lands farther to the west.

In the early 1700s, groups of European settlers built villages along the Potomac River. Georgetown was officially founded in 1751, on the Maryland side of the river. South of Georgetown, the village of Hamburgh was settled near the marshy riverfront area known today as Foggy Bottom. South of the Potomac River, the village of Alexandria was established in 1749.

Georgetown was officially founded in 1751. It was one of several European villages built along the Potomac River in the 1700s.

George Washington and architect Pierre L'Enfant picked out the location of the nation's capital in 1791.

At the end of the Revolutionary War (1775-1783), the United States won its independence from Great Britain. Cities such as Philadelphia, Pennsylvania, served as temporary capitals of the new nation. In 1790, Congress decided that a permanent capital should be built on federal government land, and not be part of any state. Lawmakers compromised and decided that the capital should be built somewhere between the Northern and Southern states.

Congress created a 10-square-mile (26-sq-km) district along the shores of the Potomac River. President George Washington picked the final location. Both Maryland and Virginia gave up land to create the new capital.

During the War of 1812, British troops entered Washington, DC, and set fire to the White House. President and Dolley Madison had already fled the city.

The nation's federal government moved to Washington in 1800. At first, the city suffered hard times. Many did not like its location. Summers were too hot and humid, and there was too much marshland nearby. In 1814, during the War of 1812 (1812-1815), the British army captured and burned part of the city, including the White House and the Capitol. (The buildings were quickly rebuilt.) During the Civil War (1861-1865), the city was threatened several times by the Confederate army.

In 1847, the federal government returned the land south of the Potomac River to the state of Virginia. The city of Alexandria was included. In 1871, the city of Washington absorbed Georgetown and other small communities within the District of Columbia. The capital became commonly known as Washington, DC.

1888 Building the Library of Congress

1890

1892

1894

2016

In the late 1800s and early 1900s, many of the city's most famous buildings and stone monuments were built, which brought much world attention. The structures included the Library of Congress, the Lincoln Memorial, and the towering Washington Monument.

By 1900, more than 250,000 people lived in Washington, DC. The city was growing much faster than expected. World War I (1914-1918) and World War II (1939-1945) saw rapid expansions of government programs and the military. The government was forced to hire many new workers, which caused the city to grow even more.

Dr. Martin Luther King, Jr. was a civil rights leader in the 1950s and 1960s. He gave his famous "I have a dream" speech to a crowd of about 250,000 freedom marchers at the nation's capital on August 28, 1963.

Washington continued to grow in the first part of the 20th century. New government buildings, monuments, and museums were built, along with train stations and roads. Sometimes, progress was not easy to achieve. African Americans lived in the city, but they suffered from terrible discrimination, like a lot of blacks around the country. On August 28, 1963, Dr. Martin Luther King, Jr. gave his powerful "I have a dream" speech from the steps of the Lincoln Memorial in front of 250,000 people. New civil rights laws in the 1950s and 1960s helped ease discrimination.

The city continued to grow as the federal government expanded. By 1950, Washington's population had ballooned to 800,000. Unfortunately, the city's rapid growth caused big headaches. By the late 1900s, city services had grown old, and the federal government had not provided enough money to fix the problems.

The citizens of Washington, DC, do not have the same rights as people in the 50 states of the Union. They are not represented by lawmakers in Congress, although they can vote for president. In 1975, the people gained the right to elect their own mayor and city council. Unfortunately, in the years to come, much of the city's finances were mismanaged or wasted. Poverty, drug addiction, and homelessness were big problems. Many people left to live in neighboring suburbs in Maryland or Virginia.

A homeless man sleeps on a steam grate near the White House in 1990.

In 1995, Congress created a special group that oversaw the finances of the city. The supervision stopped in 2001 after Washington balanced its budgets. Like most big cities, Washington continues to struggle against crime and poverty. But many parts of the city have greatly improved. Today, more and more people enjoy Washington's culture, history, and fine quality of life.

PEOPLE

Duke Ellington (1899-1974) was a composer, pianist, and bandleader. He was one of the most famous jazz musicians of the 1900s. Born in Washington, DC, he started taking piano lessons at age seven. He quickly became an expert in several musical styles. He started performing with his first band in 1917, playing in the Washington, DC, area. He became known by his nickname, "The Duke." Ellington gained most of his fame in the 1930s and 1940s, but continued playing and recording music until the mid-1970s. He and his band played jazz, big band, ragtime, swing, and other styles. He wrote much music, often combining musical styles. His band toured the United States and other countries from the 1920s until his death in 1974.

Dr. Charles Drew (1904-1950) was a surgeon who was born and grew up in Washington, DC. He was a student athlete who became interested in medicine. Despite roadblocks he faced as an African American, he quickly became an outstanding surgeon and research scientist.

In the 1930s and 1940s, he discovered new ways to safely test and store blood, and how to organize blood donors. The blood could then be used in large-scale hospital blood banks to help accident victims and wounded soldiers. Blood banks saved many lives during World War II (1939-1945). Drew directed blood bank programs in the United States and Great Britain through the war years. He later resigned because of the military's policy of segregating blood donated by African Americans. Drew went on to become the chief surgeon at Freedmen's Hospital (later Howard University Hospital) in Washington, DC.

John Philip Sousa (1854-1932) was a famous band conductor and composer. Born and raised in Washington, DC, he studied music as a child. He learned to play many instruments, including the violin, trombone, piano, and flute. He became the conductor of the United States Marine Corps band in 1880, which made Sousa famous worldwide. He left the Marine Corps in 1892 to conduct his own band and to continue writing music. Sousa was known as "The March King." His most famous compositions include "Stars and Stripes Forever" (the official march of the United States), "Semper Fidelis" (the official march of the Marine Corps), and "The Liberty Bell." Sousa also helped develop the sousaphone, a marching band instrument similar to a tuba.

Bill Nye (1955-) is a mechanical engineer who became one of the most famous science educators in the country. Born and raised in Washington, DC, he grew interested in science at an early age. He earned a college degree in mechanical engineering in 1977, then taught astronomy and ecology. He began appearing on television shows, demonstrating science experiments. He starred in *Bill Nye the Science Guy* from 1993 to 1998 on PBS Kids. Nye became famous for the fun way he taught science lessons, as well as for his trademark blue lab coat and bow tie. Today, Nye continues to teach, making appearances on television and radio programs all over the country. He also conducts research. Nye helped develop a sundial and camera calibrator that was attached to the *Spirit* and *Opportunity* Mars rovers.

THE NATIONAL MALL

The most popular and well-known landmark in the nation's capital is the **National Mall**. It is a long parkway in downtown Washington, DC. Some of the country's most important buildings are located there, including the United States Capitol, the Washington Monument, and the Lincoln Memorial.

The National Mall was first imagined by architect Pierre L'Enfant. His vision came to life in the early 1900s, when Congress set aside funding to create a wide, grassy parkway, with roadways and elm trees on either side. The strip of land stretches almost 2 miles (3.2 km) long. It covers about 300 acres (121 ha) of parkland. The Washington Monument is almost at the mall's center.

The parkway is part of the National Mall and Memorial Parks unit of the National Park Service. It includes the mall and many important monuments and buildings surrounding it. The following pages highlight some of the most famous.

The **Lincoln Memorial** honors Abraham Lincoln, the 16th president of the United States. It is located on the very western edge of the National Mall. The building is made of white Yule marble from Colorado. It resembles an ancient Greek temple, with 36 tall columns ringing the outer walls (one for each state at the time of Lincoln's death in 1865). Inside is a colossal statue of President Lincoln seated in a chair. Made of white Georgia

marble, the statue was carved by seven members of the Piccirilli family and supervised by sculptor Daniel Chester French. It is 19 feet (6 m) tall, from the top of Lincoln's head to his feet. It weighs 175 tons (159 metric tons). The Lincoln Memorial was dedicated in 1922.

The **Washington Monument** is almost in the center of the National Mall. Made of white marble, granite, and bluestone gneiss, it is shaped like an ancient Egyptian obelisk. It soars nearly 555 feet (169 m) high. The monument honors George Washington, the first president of the United States. Construction began in 1848, but it remained unfinished for many years because of a lack of funds and the Civil War (1861-1865). The monument was finally completed in 1884. At that time, it was the tallest structure in the world, until the Eiffel Tower was built in Paris, France, the following year. Today, elevators whisk visitors to an observation deck near the top of the tower for breathtaking views of the city.

Work ceased on the Washington Monument, in 1854, leaving it unfinished for decades.

The **National World War II Memorial** honors the "Greatest Generation," those Americans who served during World

War II (1939-1945). It is located on the mall, just west of the Washington Monument. Dedicated in 2004, the memorial features fountains, arches, and 56 granite pillars arranged in a semicircle. On the west side of the memorial is the Freedom Wall. It displays 4,048 gold stars. Each star represents 100 Americans who died fighting in the war.

The **Vietnam Veterans Memorial** is near the Lincoln Memorial, on the west side of the mall. It is made of two granite walls, set at an angle. The

walls are engraved with the names of more than 58,000 Americans who lost their lives fighting in the Vietnam War (1955-1975). Many people come to find the name of family or friends and make a paper rubbing of the name as a memento.

The **National Archives Building** is very close to the National Mall, on Constitution Avenue. It safely stores thousands of historic documents. Original copies of the Declaration of Independence, the Constitution, and the Bill of Rights are on display in the building's rotunda. Other important documents include the Emancipation Proclamation and the Louisiana Purchase Treaty.

The National Museum of Natural History

The National Air and Space Museum

The **Smithsonian Institution** is nicknamed "the Nation's Attic." Founded in 1846, it preserves more than 138 million items relating to science, art, and history. The objects are contained in 19 different museums. Many of them are located on the National Mall. The two most popular are the National Museum of Natural History, and the National Air and Space Museum.

The **United States Capitol** building is on the far eastern end of the National Mall. Members of Congress meet in the Capitol to make laws. The north wing of the Capitol houses the U.S. Senate. The south wing houses the U.S. House of Representatives. In the middle of the Capitol is a rotunda. It is a large circular room covered by a 180-foot (55-m) inner dome. The Capitol is filled with many paintings, sculptures, and other historic artwork.

THE
WHITE HOUSE

The White House is the place where the president of the United States lives and works. Its famous address in Washington, DC, is 1600 Pennsylvania Avenue. It is just north of the National Mall.

In 1792, President George Washington chose James Hoban to be the building's chief architect. Workers began construction in October 1792, using sandstone from Virginia quarries.

In 1800, after eight years of construction, President John Adams moved into the White House. He only lived there a short time. Thomas Jefferson, the third president of the United States, was the first president to live in the White House from the beginning of his term.

President Obama in the Oval Office.

Over the years, the White House has had several names, including the President's House, the President's Palace, and the Executive Mansion. In 1901, President Theodore Roosevelt gave the White House its current official name.

The White House has six levels. Four are above ground, and two are underground. There is 55,000 square feet (5,110 sq m) of floor space, which includes 132 rooms, 35 bathrooms, and 28 fireplaces. There is also a tennis court, a swimming pool, a movie theater, and a bowling lane.

The president does not own the White House. It is owned by the citizens of the United States. Many parts of the building are open to the public for tours. About 100,000 people visit the White House each month.

THE CHERRY TREES

O ne of the most popular gatherings in Washington, DC, is the two-week National Cherry Blossom Festival. Each spring, more than 3,750 cherry trees bloom, splashing the city with shades of soft white and vivid pink. The trees are located in several spots, from the Tidal Basin near the Potomac River, to the National Mall near the Washington Monument.

In 1909, the mayor of Tokyo, Japan, gave 2,000 cherry trees to the United States, to be planted in the nation's capital. In Japan, the cherry tree is an important flowering plant. The gift was meant to symbolize the lasting friendship between the people of Japan and the United States.

PHOTO BY ZACH BREWER, WASHINGTON, D. C.

72171 JAPANESE CHERRY BLOSSOMS, RIVERSIDE DRIVE, POTOMAC RIVER, WASHINGTON, D. C.

A postcard from the 1900s shows cherry trees near the Washington Monument.

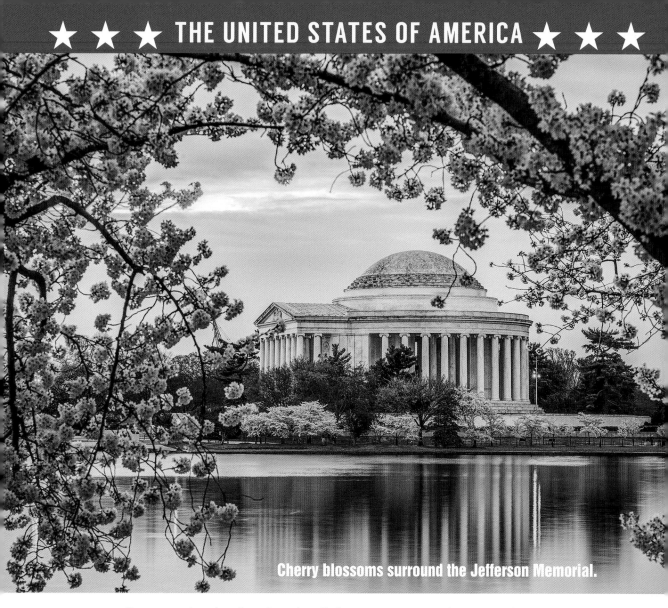

Cherry blossoms surround the Jefferson Memorial.

Unfortunately, the first batch of cherry trees was discovered to be infested with harmful insect pests and plant diseases. The trees were burned to keep the infestation from spreading. In 1912, Japan donated another 3,000 trees. First Lady Helen Taft and the wife of the Japanese ambassador planted the first two cherry trees near the Tidal Basin.

In 1927, schoolchildren began reenacting the 1912 tree planting. Within a few years, the National Cherry Blossom Festival grew into an annual celebration. Today, more than 1.5 million people come each year to witness the beauty of Washington's cherry trees in bloom.

THE CHERRY TREES

THE SMITHSONIAN
NATIONAL ZOO

The Smithsonian National Zoological Park is one of the oldest zoos in the United States. It was founded in 1889 when Congress passed a law creating a national zoo "for the advancement of science and the instruction and recreation of the people." The following year, the zoo became part of the Smithsonian Institution.

Commonly called the National Zoo, the 163-acre (66-ha) public park is located just north of downtown. It is home to more than 2,000 animals from almost 400 species. Many of the animals are endangered. The zoo is one of the city's most popular tourist destinations. More than 2 million people visit each year. The zoo is open 364 days per year, and admission is free.

Many visitors come to see the National Zoo's most famous residents: Tian Tian, Mei Xiang, Bao Bao, and Bei Bei. They are endangered giant pandas on loan to the zoo from China.

Giant pandas Mei Xiang (left) and Tian Tian (right) at the National Zoo. It is one of only four zoos in the United States where giant pandas can be seen.

Cheetahs

Western Lowland Gorillas

Asian Elephants

Besides giant pandas, the National Zoo is home to other mammals such as African lions, American bison, gray wolves, Asian elephants, cheetahs, and western lowland gorillas. The zoo also has hundreds of species of amphibians, birds, fish, and reptiles. In addition to housing and exhibiting animals, the National Zoo performs scientific animal research at its 3,200-acre (1,295-ha) campus near Front Royal, Virginia.

THE SMITHSONIAN NATIONAL ZOO

TRANSPORTATION

There are 1,501 miles (2,416 km) of public roadways in Washington, DC. Traffic is often very heavy in the city. Many people choose to take public transportation to get to work. Many others walk or ride bicycles.

The Metrorail is a train and subway system that serves the city and the surrounding area. Most people simply call it "the Metro." Inside the city, it mainly operates as a subway. In the surrounding suburbs, the tracks run on or above the surface. More than 836,000 commuters use the Metro each weekday. That makes it one of the busiest rapid transit systems in the country.

Thousands of commuters load and unload at Metrorail train stations every day.

Reagan National Airport handles more than 21 million passengers each year.

Several Amtrak lines and other commuter train lines serve Washington, DC. Travelers are whisked from neighboring states directly into the city. Union Station is a major hub for trains in downtown Washington. First opened in 1907, today it is one of the busiest stations in the nation, serving more than 90,000 people each day.

Three major airports serve the Washington, DC, area. The closest to the downtown area is Ronald Reagan Washington National Airport. It is located across the Potomac River in Arlington County, Virginia. Commonly called Reagan National, it handles more than 21 million fliers yearly. Other major airports that serve the city include Washington Dulles International Airport, in Virginia, and Baltimore-Washington International Thurgood Marshall Airport, which is located in Maryland.

INDUSTRY

I t is no surprise that the single biggest employer in the Washington, DC, metropolitan area is the federal government. The government hires hundreds of thousands of people to run the nation's business. Many other people work for companies that serve the government in some way. There are also a lot of people who work for lobbying firms that represent companies or trade associations. They try to convince lawmakers to pass legislation that would be good for their businesses.

Many people work at the Capitol and in nearby congressional office buildings in Washington, DC. The federal government is the area's biggest employer.

Tourists on Segways and on foot tour the National Mall in Washington, DC.

Many Washington, DC, workers are employed in the service industry. Instead of making products, service industry companies sell services to other consumers, or to the government. It includes businesses such as health care, insurance, advertising, financial services, and marketing.

One very important service industry in Washington, DC, is tourism. People come from all over the country to see historic landmarks such as the Washington Monument and museums such as the Smithsonian Institution. Each year, more than 20 million visitors spend about $6.8 billion in Washington, DC. That is enough to support more than 74,000 jobs.

There is a small amount of manufacturing in Washington, DC. Printing and food products are important. There are also jobs in construction and high-technology industries.

SPORTS

Washington, DC, has several professional major league sports teams to cheer for. The Washington Redskins play in the National Football League (NFL). The team has won the Super Bowl three times, most recently for the 1991 season. The Washington Nationals are a Major League Baseball (MLB) team. They began playing in the city in 2005, and have won two National League East Division titles.

The Washington Wizards shoot hoops in the National Basketball Association (NBA). They won the NBA Championship in 1978 (the team's name at that time was the Washington Bullets). The Washington Capitals skate in the National Hockey League (NHL). The Washington Mystics play in the Women's National Basketball Association (WNBA). D.C. United is a Major League Soccer (MLS) team. It has won four MLS Cup championships.

Teams of rowers move their boats across the Potomac River. Water sports of all kinds are popular in the Washington, DC, area.

College sports are closely followed in the Washington, DC, area. Basketball is very popular. The Georgetown Hoyas, the men's team from Georgetown University, is often one of the top-ranked teams in the nation. They won the NCAA Men's Division I Basketball Tournament in 1984.

Because the climate of Washington, DC, is mild, outdoor sports are very popular. There are many parks in which to play softball, volleyball, and other sports. Major running marathons are held in the city. Water sports are also popular, including swimming, sailing, and rowing.

Jack the Bulldog is a mascot for the Georgetown Hoyas.

ENTERTAINMENT

Washington, DC, is filled with museums, theaters, and historic places to visit. The Smithsonian Institution was created by Congress in 1846. Its mission is to preserve the nation's history and knowledge. Its 19 museums are visited by millions of people each year. The National Museum of Natural History is on the National Mall. It contains millions of specimens of animals, plants, rocks, and fossils. The National Air and Space Museum is also on the National Mall. It displays dozens of historic aircraft and spacecraft, including the *Spirit of St. Louis* (the first plane to be flown solo nonstop across the Atlantic Ocean) and the Apollo 11 Command Module *Columbia*, which carried the first astronauts to land on the Moon.

The Apollo 11 Command Module Columbia, which carried Neil Armstrong, Buzz Aldrin, and Michael Collins to the Moon in 1969, is on display at the National Air and Space Museum.

A tour group views the National Portrait Gallery's 1796 portrait of George Washington by artist Gilbert Stuart.

The National Portrait Gallery includes historical paintings of many famous Americans, including presidents such as George Washington. The National Gallery of Art has one of the finest collections of paintings, photographs, and sculptures in the world.

The United States Holocaust Memorial Museum tells the story of the millions of Jews and others who were murdered in Nazi Germany during World War II (1939-1945). Touring the artifacts and exhibitions is a very educational and moving experience.

Washington, DC, is also home to many world-class performing arts institutions. They include the National Symphony Orchestra, the Washington Ballet, the Washington National Opera, and the John F. Kennedy Center for the Performing Arts.

ENTERTAINMENT

TIMELINE

Pre-1700s—Piscataway and Powhatan Native Americans settle in the Washington, DC, area.

1751—The settlement of Georgetown founded.

1790—The United States Congress passes a law to create a site for a new permanent capital.

1791—President George Washington picks the final location for the new national capital, a 10-square-mile (26-sq-km) district along the shores of the Potomac River. The states of Maryland and Virginia give up lands to create the capital.

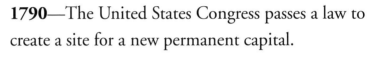

1793—Construction of the Capitol building begins.

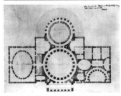

1800—The federal government moves to Washington, DC.

1814—British soldiers burn many city buildings during the War of 1812.

1847—Part of the District of Columbia land is returned to Virginia.

1861–1865—The Civil War breaks out. Union troops protect the city from Confederate forces.

1884—Construction of the Washington Monument is completed.

1922—The Lincoln Memorial is dedicated.

1943—The Jefferson Memorial is dedicated.

1963—Dr. Martin Luther King, Jr. gives his "I have a dream" speech from the steps of the Lincoln Memorial in front of 250,000 people.

2001—Five terrorists hijack and fly a plane into the Pentagon, just across the Potomac River in Arlington County, Virginia, on September 11, killing 184 innocent people.

2009—President Barack Obama, the first African American president, moves into the White House.

2015—The Georgetown University Hoyas men's basketball team makes its 30th appearance at the NCAA Division I Tournament.

GLOSSARY

Architect
A person who creates the plans to make something, such as a building or a city.

Civil War
The war fought between America's Northern and Southern states from 1861-1865. The Southern states were for slavery. They wanted to start their own country. Northern states fought against slavery and a division of the country.

District of Columbia
A piece of land set aside to house the federal government.

Emancipation Proclamation
President Abraham Lincoln's declaration that set free those slaves in states that were still in rebellion against the Union during the Civil War.

Infest
To be full of large numbers of insects or other pests, which often cause damage to other nearby living things.

Louisiana Purchase
A purchase by the United States from France in 1803 of a huge section of land west of the Mississippi River. The United States nearly doubled in size after the purchase. The young country paid $15 million for approximately 828,000 square miles (2.1 million sq km) of land.

Obelisk
A tall, narrow, four-sided monument with a pyramid shape on top.

Reservoir

A lake, either man-made or natural, that is often used as a source of water for a nearby city.

Revolutionary War

The war fought between the American colonies and Great Britain from 1775-1783. It is also known as the American Revolution or the War of Independence.

Rotunda

A circularly shaped building, often covered with a dome. The United States Capitol building in Washington, DC, features a central rotunda section.

Rubbing

Taking an impression of something by placing a piece of paper on top of the design, then using a crayon or pencil to rub over the paper. People often take rubbings of names carved into the Vietnam Veterans Memorial.

Smithsonian Institution

An organization created by Congress in 1846 to maintain the nation's official museums and galleries. There are several Smithsonian-run museums located in Washington, DC. They are very popular tourist destinations.

Tidal Basin

In Washington, DC, the Tidal Basin is a man-made reservoir near the Potomac River and the Washington Channel. Many cherry trees grow around it. The Jefferson Memorial is next to the Tidal Basin.

INDEX